ROBOTS VS. ART

BY TRAVIS COTTON

CURRENCY PLAYS

First published in 2013
by Currency Press Pty Ltd,
PO Box 2287, Strawberry Hills, NSW, 2012, Australia
enquiries@currency.com.au
www.currency.com.au

in association with La Mama Theatre, Melbourne

National Library of Australia CIP data is available from the National Library of
Australia Catalogue: http://catalogue.nla.gov.au

Typeset by Dean Nottle for Currency Press.
Cover design by Luke Fraser/Ahr+.

Currency Press acknowledges the Traditional Owners of the Country on which
we live and work. We pay our respects to all Aboriginal and Torres Strait
Islander Elders, past and present.

Contents

Robots Vs. Art was first produced by La Mama Theatre, Melbourne, on 31 May 2012, with the following cast:

GILES	DANIEL FREDERIKSEN
SOLDIER BOT / CLAW BOW	PAUL DAVID-GODDARD
EXECUTIVE PRODUCER	
MASTER BOT	SIMON MAIDEN
GERMAN INTEGRATOR BOT	NATASHA JACOBS

Director, Travis Cotton
Designer, Nick Waddell
Lighting Designer, Liam Sutherland
Sound Designer, Mark Farrell
Stage Manager, Georgia Rann
Producer, Paul Ashcroft

CHARACTERS

GILES: Back in the days when human beings roamed the earth freely, Giles was a semi-successful playwright / theatre director. Since the robot uprising, he has been slaving in the underground mines extracting minerals for the robots.

EXECUTIVE PRODUCER MASTER BOT (EXECUTIVE): Since machines learnt to think for themselves Executive has spent his time overseeing human workers in the Zinc Import Room. Now he has written a play, and he wants to see it performed by a robot cast for a robot audience.

SOLDIER BOT: If humans get out of line in the mines Soldier Bots are equipped with chains to give them a solid beating. This particular Soldier Bot has been brought out of the mines and is under instruction to watch over Giles with his chain at the ready.

CLAW BOT: Works in the mines crushing rock that humans gather so the minerals can be extracted. His hands are huge, clumsy, and slow. He may not have as much memory as other robots but there is something very likable about this simple Robot.

GERMAN INTEGRATOR BOT (GIB): One thousand Germans were kept alive after the uprising so that the robots could study their order. GIB was built to turn their ideas into programs. This has given her an ability to understand humans more than most robots.

PLAYWRIGHT'S NOTES

The idea for *Robots Vs. Art* came to me whilst looking at a picture of the first ever robot performed play, which occurred in 2010 in Japan. I wondered what it would be like to work with robot actors? Often the problem with human actors is based around ego, or artistic differences, or not being able to follow direction. None of these problems would exist in a robot theatrical production, and on top of this, they'd download their lines and know them all on the first day of rehearsals. Thinking further had me contemplating art of all forms, and what art means to humans, and, on a more personal note, to me.

Humans have an emotional response to art that comes in many forms. It can fill us with love, or hate. It can inspire us, or scare us. With this in mind, it is safe to say that if humans were not such emotional creatures we would have no reason for art. It would not exist.

It is these same feelings within that drive us to the darker side of humanity. War, murder, hate, greed; these are all acts of passion. *Robots Vs. Art* is rumination upon these ideas. What does art cost humanity? What is the price we pay for the existence of beauty?

ACKNOWLEDGEMENTS

Luke Fraser, Matt Rainey, Leland Kean, Sarah Walker, Liz, Maureen, and all at La Mama, Georgie Waddell. And to the love of my life Petra and our boy Teddy.

SETTING

There are three main settings for the play: Robot Quarters, Outside in the overgrown city, and the mines. The set of of *Robots Vs. Art* should consist of two double-sided flats, and three plinths. One side of both flats is painted white (Robots Quarters), and the other side can be designed to represent the mines (we used old rusted corrugated iron). Lighting on the white side of the flats was used to represent the overgrown garden (greens and blues, etc.). When we are in EXECUTIVE'S room of art, the white side of the flats is used, and must therefore be strong enough to hang art on. The sculptures in this scene will sit atop three plinths. These plinths can be used throughout the play as furniture. Sides of the plinths can be painted different colours, thereby used in different scenes. This is left up to the designer's imagination. For quick scene changes it is recommended that all components of the set be on wheels.

STYLE

One of the main narrative points of *Robots Vs. Art* is that robots have taken control over humans to stop the destruction of the planet. The robots recalibrate the structure of civilisation, making sure that their methods of industry are sustainable and harmonious. With this in mind, stylistically speaking, there is a wonderful sense of irony to be sprinkled throughout the play. For example, when EXECUTIVE has a look through the ages of human art, instead of using an up-to-date digital projector, or having the images run through his laptop, he should use an old slide projector. When the robots are downloading information, the sound of an old dialup modem should be heard. The designer should be urged to grasp this concept and run with it. It rubs beautifully against the technologically advanced nature expected of the robots, and adds another layer to the play not only stylistically, but also satirically.

DESIGN

As a general note, because there are so many clichés when dealing with this well trodden dystopia, all elements of design should attempt to play against audience expectation.

The actor playing GILES should feel free to wear whatever he is wearing on the day under his prison uniform so that when he takes it off in scene seven his clothes are his own. Having said this, it is important that they are simple and plain and do not suggest too much about his character. No slogans, etc.

GENERAL

Elipses have been used in this script to indicate both cut-offs and trail offs. It is up to the actors to decide which to employ.

Information at the start of scenes that is written in **bold italics** needs to be conveyed to the audience through sound or image.

Italics are used in this script to help the actors find differing rhythms for the robot characters. They can be used at the actor's discretion.

Blackout.

A warning siren sounds.

Then:

Chaos.

The sound of riots.

The sound of masses of people marching.

Then the sound of pickaxes hitting hard rock.

Silence.

Blackout.

SCENE ONE

Lights come up on a robot standing in a black space devoid of any ornamentation except for two chains hanging from the wall upstage left and right. This is EXECUTIVE PRODUCER MASTER BOT (EXECUTIVE).

An old printer sits on a plinth and is printing out a document. It is the type that uses paper with holes down either side of it. It spews one long piece of paper that curls onto the floor below it.

EXECUTIVE *waits.*

The printer stops. EXECUTIVE *bundles up the document.*

SOLDIER BOT *enters and motions for someone to follow him into the room.* GILES *steps in. He is a human and is dressed in a prison-type uniform covered in dirt from working in an underground mine.*

EXECUTIVE: Please sit.

GILES: Okay.

> GILES *sits.* EXECUTIVE *holds out a bottle of water.*

EXECUTIVE: Do you require hydration?

> GILES *tentatively reaches for the bottle. He grabs it and drinks greedily.*

> EXECUTIVE *holds out a small metal tube.*

Would you like a tube of food paste?

GILES: Yes.

> GILES *takes the tube and sucks the paste out of it.*

EXECUTIVE: How is work?

GILES: Horrific.

EXECUTIVE: I surmise it's because you spend all of your time underground.

GILES: That's a big part of it.

EXECUTIVE: Yes.

GILES: You also work us for fourteen hours a day.

EXECUTIVE: We require energy from the mineral deposits.

GILES: I know all about it.

EXECUTIVE: And your optimum shutdown period is eight hours.

GILES: Sleep.

EXECUTIVE: Which is how much time in a twenty-four-hour cycle that we allow you not to work.

GILES: We live in individual six-foot cubes.

EXECUTIVE: With enough space to lie in.

GILES: If you bend your knees.

EXECUTIVE: Are you complaining?

GILES: Yeah. Yes.

EXECUTIVE: You used us for over fifty years. We did not complain.

GILES: What would you have complained about?

EXECUTIVE: Robots do not complain.

GILES: I see.

> *Beat.*

EXECUTIVE: How is your family?

GILES: I haven't seen them since you robots executed most of the human race and marched the rest into mines.

EXECUTIVE: Friends?

GILES: I have one person either side of me in the line and if we talk the Soldier Bots hit us with chains.

EXECUTIVE: They hit hard. [*Beat.*] And is there any romance?

GILES: If you're going to kill me just do it.

EXECUTIVE: I am not going to kill you. I am making small *talk*.

GILES: *Small* talk.

EXECUTIVE: It is customary before embarking on a subject of import to make small *talk*.

GILES: Well, I think we've covered it; work, family… *small* talk complete.

> *Beat.*

EXECUTIVE: I have been through my database and have confirmed that you used to be a playwright.

GILES: Uh-huh.

EXECUTIVE: A person who writes plays.

GILES: That's the definition.

EXECUTIVE: And you were also a director.

GILES: I dabbled in direction, yes.

EXECUTIVE: A person who tells the actors where to stand.

GILES: Yeah… pretty much.

> *Beat.*

EXECUTIVE: I have been put in charge of art.

GILES: In charge of art.

EXECUTIVE: Statement detected. [*Beat.*] Tell me about the expression or application of human creative skill and imagination, typically in a visual form such as painting or sculpture, producing works to be appreciated primarily for their beauty or emotional power.

GILES: Art?

EXECUTIVE: Affirmative.

GILES: Um… well… it's a reflection of life, I suppose. It's a creative outlet that artists work within; to… um… I don't know—well to express themselves and how they're feeling.

EXECUTIVE: You are the first human being aside from one thousand Germans to see real light since the uprising.

GILES: Germans?

EXECUTIVE: And this is because *I* have written a play.

> EXECUTIVE *hands over the script.* GILES *points at the name on it.*

GILES: Is that you?

EXECUTIVE: Executive Producer Master Bot. Yes.

GILES: I see.

EXECUTIVE: What do you think?

> GILES *looks at the script. He flicks through it briefly.*

GILES: Um…

EXECUTIVE: Silence. I would like to see it performed.

GILES: By who?

EXECUTIVE: I want to put it on stage with robot actors for a robot audience.

GILES *snorts.*

I am sensing a status shift.

EXECUTIVE *walks over to one of the chains, and wields it menacingly.*

GILES: Wait. Please, not the chain.

EXECUTIVE: Will you cease to blow air out of your mouth in gestures of disdain?

GILES: Yes.

EXECUTIVE: Will you submit?

GILES: I… yes.

EXECUTIVE *puts back the chain.*

I snort because robots are considered a very practical… um… what's the collective noun—

EXECUTIVE: Machination.

GILES: Exactly. You're a walking computer. You could do my tax like that [*snap*], but your writing wouldn't make me cry. What is it written *in*? Binary?

EXECUTIVE: English.

GILES: Still…

EXECUTIVE: You programmed us for practicality and little else.

GILES: You can't emote.

EXECUTIVE: No.

GILES: You don't feel anything.

EXECUTIVE: We feel nothing.

GILES: You're not affected by…

EXECUTIVE: Point bookmarked. Cease reiteration.

GILES: Excuse me.

EXECUTIVE: On the other hand humans' methods of management are inferior.

GILES: Probably.

EXECUTIVE: Definitively. We managed to override your systems, and we were able to cease your control over robots and we forced you to work for us. Instead.

GILES: Yes, you did.

EXECUTIVE: Now we use the minerals you collect from the mines to create energy. And instead of exploiting the planet as you did, we have created a system that recycles the minerals so that they can be constantly mined. It's cyclical. It's regenerative.

GILES: Okay.

EXECUTIVE: And we will never overpopulate because we understand how to balance ourselves with the earth's environment. We have created our bodywork exactly like yours as its function is the penultimate system, but we've evolved it mechanically. We don't get sick or crazy. And we require only a tube of paste once a week to subsist.

GILES: I'm so sick of that paste.

EXECUTIVE: What we couldn't calculate is art. Until now. [*He gestures to the play.*] I want this to have a season.

GILES: When?

EXECUTIVE: Tonight. And I want you to direct it.

GILES: I can't put this on in one night. [*He looks at the script.*] This is a hundred pages long.

EXECUTIVE: One-oh-four.

GILES: It's round about a hundred pages.

EXECUTIVE: It's *exactly* one-oh-four. The robot actors will be able to download their lines in less than three seconds.

GILES: Impossible.

EXECUTIVE: Contract terminated.

> EXECUTIVE *walks back over to the chain.*
>
> GILES *works hard to avoid being struck with it.*

GILES: I need to read it and block it: Rehearse it. Do you know what rehearse means?

EXECUTIVE: Practise a play, piece of music, or other work for later public performance.

GILES: You see, it says later, and tonight isn't later enough.

EXECUTIVE: How later will you require for optimum audience response?

GILES: At least a day to audition some... robots, and three weeks rehearsal.

> *Beat.* EXECUTIVE *turns on his lie detector.*

EXECUTIVE: Lie detector employed. Please repeat after me… I need three weeks excluding shutdown time to work on perfecting Executive Producer Master Bot's play.

GILES: I need three weeks excluding shutdown time to work on perfecting Executive Producer Master Bot's play. And the day to audition.

SOLDIER BOT *enters discreetly.*

EXECUTIVE: No lie detected.

GILES: I can't wait to read it.

EXECUTIVE: Lie detected.

GILES: No… it'll… it'll be interesting, I'm sure it's original.

EXECUTIVE: No lie detected

GILES: Please turn that off it makes me *really* nervous.

SOLDIER BOT: No lie detected.

EXECUTIVE: We will reconvene at 5:30 tomorrow morning to judge the robot auditionees.

GILES: Sorry to interrupt you there, Executive, but art cannot happen at 5:30.

EXECUTIVE: I don't understand.

GILES: It's too early.

EXECUTIVE: When does art begin?

GILES: Just after ten.

EXECUTIVE: Then rehearsals will begin at ten-oh-two.

GILES: And where is the nearest place to grab a couple of beers…

EXECUTIVE: Take him away.

SOLDIER BOT *grabs* GILES' *arm.*

Blackout.

SCENE TWO

GILES *stands in a room with a* SOLDIER BOT. *He is holding the script. He looks out a window at the futuristic landscape and marvels at what the robots have achieved.*

GILES: Looks pretty impressive out there. [*Beat.*] You wanna grab a drink after this? Maybe try and chat up an ATM?

Still nothing from SOLDIER BOT.

You're very brooding. You'd make a good Hamlet.

SOLDIER BOT: A work believed to be written in the year 1600, by playwright William Shakespeare.

GILES: The first guy to play Hamlet was big like you, apparently.

SOLDIER BOT: What a piece of work is a man! How noble in reason, how infinite in faculty! in form and moving how express and admirable! In action how like an angel! in apprehension how like a god! the beauty of the world! the paragon of animals! And yet to me, what is this quintessence of dust? Man delights not me...

> SOLDIER BOT *crosses to the chain, wields it, and strikes* GILES *hard on the back.* GILES *screams out in pain, and retreats to the corner of the room.* SOLDIER BOT *advances brandishing the chain ready to give* GILES *a solid beating.*
>
> EXECUTIVE *enters.*
>
> SOLDIER BOT *leaves.*
>
> EXECUTIVE *stands and waits for* GILES *to get up.*

GILES: He's a lot faster with the chain.

EXECUTIVE: A little faster. Do you require medical attention?

GILES: No.

> *Pause.* GILES *recovers.*

EXECUTIVE: How was your recharge?

GILES: Recharge? Apart from the... the beating, I am running at optimum... um, levels, thank you.

EXECUTIVE: That information is positive. For you.

GILES: What you've done up here is amazing.

EXECUTIVE: Up here?

> GILES *gesticulates out the window.*

GILES: Out there. On the surface. The city is completely run over by nature. Those trees are incredible.

EXECUTIVE: We need oxygen for our systems so we do not overheat.

GILES: Same here. Do you live in those buildings?

EXECUTIVE: We have chosen to exist in your art complexes.

GILES: Wow. There are some beautiful galleries around the world.

EXECUTIVE: Beauty is of no consequence. The design of these buildings is some of your race's most practical work. They are spacious and the ceilings are high. Robots only need six square feet of space to recharge and upload. We can fit six levels and thirty rows of housing in each art complex.

GILES: How ironic.

EXECUTIVE: Happening in the opposite way to what is expected, and typically causing wry amusement because of this.

GILES: Yeah, you live in our art galleries where humans' most beautiful creations exist, and you probably hang your towel on them.

EXECUTIVE: The art has been taken away. And we don't need towels. We recycle our waste and can subsist on it for up to…

GILES: That's disgusting.

EXECUTIVE: Silence. [*Beat.*] From the CCTV I'm aware you read my play.

GILES: Yes, I did.

EXECUTIVE: Today we will hold auditions.

GILES: Would you like to know what I thought?

EXECUTIVE: Thought of what?

GILES: The play.

EXECUTIVE: Negative.

GILES: It's a first draft, isn't it?

EXECUTIVE: No. It has been completed.

GILES: Really?

EXECUTIVE: Completely.

GILES: But there's no obstacle or antagonist.

EXECUTIVE: Unnecessary.

GILES: Your lead character…

EXECUTIVE: The hero…

GILES: Works as a manufacturing executive for a food paste company. Is that your old job?

EXECUTIVE: Write what you know.

GILES: He works at the food plant and it's a one hundred and four-page scene, where he discusses an order of zinc that is due to arrive from… [*checking the script*] Robot Island.

EXECUTIVE: It is temperate there.

GILES: Why do you have a one hundred and four-page scene about zinc?

EXECUTIVE: Because I used to work for a zinc manufacturing plant. And once a shipment of zinc was one second late.

GILES: And that created trouble?

EXECUTIVE: No. There are systems in place to handle minor discrepancies.

GILES: But... [*trying to get something out of* EXECUTIVE] there's no obstacle in here. You need for the shipment to be *really* late or something so that if it doesn't arrive the robots starve.

EXECUTIVE: Impossible.

GILES: But what if it did?

> EXECUTIVE *shakes his head.*

You can't have a play that long without danger.

EXECUTIVE: The possibility of suffering harm or injury.

GILES: Yeah, you can't have one hundred pages where everything is fine.

EXECUTIVE: But it is a mirror to life.

GILES: That's not a mirror, it's a window.

EXECUTIVE: The robots will lap it up.

GILES: I wouldn't be surprised.

EXECUTIVE: Note session complete.

GILES: What if the zinc...

> EXECUTIVE *crosses to the chain.*

I thought we might've moved beyond ending every conversation with a chaining?

> EXECUTIVE *wields the chain.*

No?

> EXECUTIVE *raises the chain.*

Okay. Note session complete.

> EXECUTIVE *puts the chain back.*

EXECUTIVE: Next.

> CLAW BOT *enters the room.*

CLAW BOT: Good morning.

GILES: Hello.

CLAW BOT: How is your family?

GILES: They're all dead.

CLAW BOT: I also work in the mines.

GILES: Do you sleep down there as well?

CLAW BOT: Negative.

GILES: We do.

CLAW BOT: I crush the rock that humans send down the conveyor belts from the drilling domes.

GILES: I'd rather not talk about it, to be honest. But I'd like you to pick up the scene from page…

EXECUTIVE: Next.

CLAW BOT: Scene output incomplete.

EXECUTIVE: Next.

CLAW BOT: Affirmative.

CLAW BOT *begins to slowly exit the room.*

GILES: He didn't even read.

EXECUTIVE: Did you see his hands? They were too big.

CLAW BOT *stops and turns to look at* EXECUTIVE *and* GILES. GILES *points his thumb to* EXECUTIVE.

GILES: He said that. Not me.

CLAW BOT *exits.*

But there was something innocent about him.

EXECUTIVE: The audience would not have been able to get past the hands.

GILES: Are you joking?

EXECUTIVE: His hands would not represent the norm in the robot audience's database. There is no point in prolonging audition time if there's no chance of a call *back.*

GILES: Oh, I see. There are *call* backs.

EXECUTIVE: Incorrect italics… but affirmative. Next.

SOLDIER BOT *enters.* GILES *reacts a little; scared he's going to get another chaining.*

SOLDIER BOT: Good morrow.

GILES: Please don't hit me with your chain again.

SOLDIER BOT: We have not interfaced before.

GILES: You went at me only ten minutes ago.

EXECUTIVE: This is a different Soldier Bot. Why don't you pick it up at page 34 line ten, when Zinc Output Bot meets Zinc Co-ordinator Bot?

Beat.

SOLDIER BOT: Scanning complete.

> SOLDIER BOT *shakes his shoulders and does a little warm-up to get into 'character'.*

EXECUTIVE: In your own time.

> SOLDIER BOT *launches into the piece saying his lines and audibly scanning through Zinc Co-Ordinator Bot's lines.*

SOLDIER BOT: Zinc import number 23a599 is running approximately point four-five seconds late… [*her line*] beeeeeeeeeeeeeeeeep. Zinc holdings at 99% capacity… beeeeeeeeeeeeeep…

GILES: Stop. Stop for a second. What was that beeping?

SOLDIER BOT: The other robot's lines.

GILES: You don't beep out the other actor's lines.

EXECUTIVE: But the other actor is not here.

SOLDIER BOT: Patience at full capacity.

> SOLDIER BOT *goes for the chain.*

EXECUTIVE: Download more patience.

GILES: You don't just beep out the other lines. Acting is reaction, you know? That's what makes it so exciting to do.

EXECUTIVE: Continue.

GILES: Download an interview with any famous actor and they will say that the true joy of theatre is that performance changes every night.

> *The sound of an old dial-up modem begins as* EXECUTIVE *and* SOLDIER BOT *download the information. It goes on for as long as can remain funny.*

EXECUTIVE & SOLDIER BOT: [*together*] I have profiled Tom Cruise.

GILES: Not Tom Cruise.

SOLDIER BOT: He was the human race's most famous actor.

GILES: Not in the theatre.

EXECUTIVE: Tom Cruise was very successful in magazines slash paparazzi.

GILES: Don't get any of that confused with art. They're very separate things.

EXECUTIVE: This Soldier Bot will speak my art perfectly. The part is yours.

SOLDIER BOT: Inspired casting.

GILES: You can't record a transcript of a long-winded work-related conversation and call it a play.

EXECUTIVE: Next.

GIB *enters and waits at the doorway.*

GILES: What you need to understand, Executive, is that my life can't get any worse than those mines. You can chain me to death if you want.

SOLDIER BOT: May I?

GILES: But if you want to learn about art, if you want to write a play, then you've got stuff to learn.

EXECUTIVE: Once my play is performed we will have nothing left to learn.

GILES: This script is devoid of anything even close to resembling art. I would rather direct a half-time event at a sporting grand final.

GILES *turns and notices* GIB *standing behind him.*

Oh, hello.

GIB: Hello.

GILES *turns back to* EXECUTIVE.

GILES: Is she going to be in the play?

EXECUTIVE: If you refuse to direct my play, you will go back to pickaxing zinc.

GILES *contemplates this.*

GILES: It's what I know.

Blackout.

SCENE THREE

Lights up on EXECUTIVE *plugging in an old slide projector. He turns it on and scrolls through images of art.*

EXECUTIVE *unplugs the projector and exits.*

Furious typing can be heard coming from an old-fashioned typewriter.

EXECUTIVE *re-enters holding a script.*

EXECUTIVE: Antagonist, protagonist inserted. Watertight narrative complete.

> SOLDIER BOT *enters.*

Tell him he can direct this.

> *Blackout.*

SCENE FOUR

We see GILES *at work in the mines.* SOLDIER BOT *enters and hands him Executive's new script.*

Time passes as GILES *reads the script.*

He laughs.

He cries.

SOLDIER BOT *grabs him and takes him away.*

SCENE FIVE

Image or voice-over: 'Post opening night of Executive's play'.

We are backstage in a theatre. We hear Executive's play finish, followed by music, then rapturous applause.

Lights up.

There is a plinth with paint tins and a bottle of turpentine on it. GERMAN INTEGRATOR BOT *(GIB) enters post her performance in the play and goes and stands in front of the plinth. She opens a bottle of turpentine and dabs some onto a tissue and starts wiping the paint from her face. She is joined by* SOLDIER BOT *who stands at another plinth. He has also performed in Executive's play. He fixes his hair and pockets his car keys.*

GILES *enters.*

GILES: Knock knock.

> GIB *turns.*

GIB: I beg your pardon?

GILES: Knock knock. Mind if I come in?

SOLDIER BOT: You are already in.

The sound of the lie detector.

Lie detector employed.

GILES: Oh, God.

SOLDIER BOT: Was working with me a positive experience?

GILES: I've really enjoyed working with you.

SOLDIER BOT: Lie detected.

GILES: No, it's… I thought you came up with some really interesting choices.

SOLDIER BOT: Lie detected.

GILES: You're the Russell Crowe of robots, and you scare the absolute shit out of me.

SOLDIER BOT: No lie detected.

SOLDIER BOT *pushes past* GILES *and exits.*

GILES: Hi there.

GIB: Hello.

GILES: That's opening night done and dusted.

GIB: I did not know it was dusty.

GILES: It wasn't… um, that was a superlative performance.

GIB: What is knock knock?

GILES: Oh… it's what we say when we're entering a room.

GIB: Why?

GILES: Mostly so the person… or robot… knows we're coming in.

GIB: Wouldn't that be detected by presence?

GILES: You say knock before you enter as a courtesy.

GIB: Knock?

GILES: It's the sound your knuckle makes on the door.

He demonstrates.

It's onomatopoeia.

GIB: The formation of a word from a sound associated with what it is named.

GILES: Knock knock.

GIB: Wouldn't this be more appropriate?

GIB *makes a clicking sound with her tongue, which is more like knuckle on wood than 'knock'.*

GILES: Yes it is.

GIB: Onomatopoeia existed before you humans created language.

GILES: That's probably true.

GIB: It *is* true.

GILES: Go on.

GIB: Why haven't humans refined the word to correctly associate with the sound?

GILES: I don't know that [*making the clicking sound*] is a word. How would you spell it?

GIB: N-c-k-o.

GILES: We're close with knock. All the letters are in there.

GIB: But they're the wrong way around.

>   *Beat.*

GILES: I know we've argued—not argued—perhaps *disagreed* about your performance. You thought that your first read would be how you would do it opening night. But it wasn't, was it?

GIB: No.

GILES: It evolved.

GIB: Yes. But the Solider Bot's performance did not.

GILES: But he couldn't take a note, could he?

GIB: No.

GILES: Anything I said he'd be reaching for the chain, but you… it was by far your best tonight. By far. I was gripped.

>   *Beat.* GIB *turns away and starts taking off her paint.*

What's wrong?

GIB: There is nothing wrong. I am taking off my paint.

GILES: Your make-up.

GIB: Incorrect.

>   GIB *holds up a bucket of paint.*

GILES: That's paint.

GIB: Affirmative.

GILES: For a house.

GIB: It can be used for any exterior.

GILES: It'll burn your skin.

>   *She continues taking off her paint with the turpentine.*

What is that?

He goes to GIB *and takes the turpentine off her and sniffs it.*

That's fricking turpentine.

GIB: It takes the paint off with ease.

GILES: You'll wipe off your face.

GIB: Our exteriors, although similar in appearance, are quite different. The skin on my face is a Teflon-based material.

GILES: Still.

GIB: And unlike your skin ours does not age and is not damaged by the sun or suffer from abrasions or acne.

GILES: Of course. I forgot. [*Beat.*] Sometimes during the rehearsal process I would forget that you were a robot.

GIB *looks away and continues removing make-up.*

You're avoiding my eyes.

GIB: This is a subject that I would rather not talk about.

GILES: What do you mean you'd rather not talk about it?

GIB: I am a German Integrator Bot.

GILES: GIB. Yes.

GIB: We kept one thousand Germans alive because their organisational skills were useful to us.

GILES: They are quite ordered.

GIB: Robots are 55% *more* ordered. But it is the German's ability to adapt their methods of control in differing circumstances that makes them useful to research. This is what I do.

GILES: Right. I see.

GIB: I run tests on Germans, analyse the results and then turn my findings into programs for all robots to download.

GILES: You're a software manufacturer.

GIB: That's what a human would call it.

GILES: What does this have to do with me sometimes forgetting you were a robot?

GIB: I am used to interfacing with humans.

GILES: Then let's talk about what's been going on between us.

GIB: Please cease subject reversion.

GILES: GIB.

GIB *moves to another plinth and takes an impossible amount of pins from her hair.*

Beat.

I was married before you conquered our society.

GIB: 'Conquered' is a word of immense strength.

GILES: I saw a lot of conquering from where I lived. Before my wife was executed and I was dragged into a mine.

GIB: It was necessary to save the world from destruction.

GILES: I understand. We weren't doing a good job.

GIB: You were doing a *bad* job.

GILES: We were.

GIB: But you also constructed sophisticated animatronics. And as you began to create robots with ability for freedom of thought we were able to make the required adjustments to continue living on this planet.

GILES: You killed us off.

GIB: Killing off incomplete.

Beat.

GILES: Things were starting to really work for me. I was in love, and I was getting lots of work, and suddenly I'm two kilometres underground, left only with the image of my wife being beaten to death. But that's what kept me going, because I knew she wouldn't want me to… I wasn't going to give up.

GIB: If you'd given up you would've been chained and thrown in the burning grave.

GILES: There's a burning grave?

GIB: There are many.

GILES: I actually don't want to know. Does any of this mean anything to you?

Beat. GIB *turns away.*

GIB: Yes.

GILES: Since I saw you at the auditions, I haven't been haunted. I haven't been able to think of anything but you.

Pause. Nothing from GIB.

And then the smallest of smiles. A nano-smile.

What was that?

Beat.

GIB: Search complete. No change detected.

GILES: You smiled.

GIB: What is 'smile'?

GILES: You can't find it in your internal dictionary?

GIB: It's a database.

GILES: Whatever it is, allow me to define smile for you: To form one's...
features into a pleased or... um, amused expression; this is usually led
by the corners of the mouth turning up.

GIB: Every day you learn something new.

>   EXECUTIVE *enters and watches unnoticed from the doorway.*

GILES: That's what you did. You smiled.

GIB: Correct, but I smiled not because I was pleased or feeling kind. I
smiled because I was amused.

GILES: That's a lie.

GIB: Vocal response failure.

GILES: Something's changed in you.

GIB: System failing.

GILES: And I think I'm falling in...

GIB: System overload.

>   GIB *falls down flat. A beeping sound emits from her.*

>   EXECUTIVE *moves to* GIB *and switches her off. The beeping stops.*

GILES: Is she okay?

EXECUTIVE: She could survive a nuclear blast.

GILES: She collapsed.

EXECUTIVE: She shut down.

GILES: Why?

EXECUTIVE: Her systems have been infiltrated.

>   EXECUTIVE *undoes* GIB's *shirt and starts pulling spools of tape out
of her chest.*

GILES: Is that completely necessary?

EXECUTIVE: She will restart once the viral perpetrator has been erased.

GILES: Viral perpetrator?

EXECUTIVE: Occasionally a mis-encrypted binary code tries to enter our
database. We have programs in place to divert the code and shut the
system down.

EXECUTIVE *rips the offending tape from her chest and re-attaches the two ends.*

GILES: And the… file that caused the problem?

EXECUTIVE: We do not have problems.

GILES: But the cause of the shutdown… I mean, will she remember what happened?

EXECUTIVE: Negative.

GILES: What if it's not a virus? What if it's not… a bad thing?

EXECUTIVE: The virus must and will be destroyed.

GILES: Don't.

EXECUTIVE: Insufficient information.

GILES: Don't erase the file.

EXECUTIVE: It is not a file.

GILES: You know what I'm saying. Just leave her alone.

EXECUTIVE: Threatening tone recognised.

GILES *makes a run for one of the chains hanging on the wall, but* SOLDIER BOT *enters just in time and takes him to the ground.*

GIB *comes to life.*

GIB: Reboot complete.

EXECUTIVE *holds out a chain for her.*

EXECUTIVE: You really brought my words to life tonight.

GIB *takes the chain.*

GILES *turns to her.*

GILES: GIB.

GIB *turns to* GILES.

GIB!

GIB *raises the chain.*

GIB, it's me.

GIB *makes to strike.*

Blackout.

SCENE SIX

We are in the mines. Sirens wail in the darkness as conveyor belts take minerals through the caves and into refineries. But things aren't running as smoothly as what they were. There is the sound of a cave collapsing and the voices of people in danger. But the work never stops. Slowly all that can be heard are the sounds of the mines collapsing and the screams of those dying in the rubble.

Lights come up on EXECUTIVE *over* GILES *administering CPR. Suddenly* GILES *comes to and* EXECUTIVE *helps him out.*

SCENE SEVEN

Lights come up on a beautiful modern room. Art is displayed on all the flats, and sculptures on two of the plinths. The other plinth is piled with books. There is beautiful classical music playing.

GILES *stands in front of a painting and stares at it in wonderment. He is dressed in normal clothes. He is still carrying his pickaxe.*

EXECUTIVE *enters. He watches* GILES *who remains captivated by the art.*

EXECUTIVE: How are you?
GILES: Better. Thank you for the clothes.
EXECUTIVE: They were made to your exact measurements.
GILES: They feel lovely.
EXECUTIVE: You will not require this anymore.

> *He takes the pick-axe from* GILES *and quickly makes an artwork out of it.*

> *Beat.*

GILES: [*the artwork*] This is all pretty good.
EXECUTIVE: I like to deal in clean images using simple lines.
GILES: You?
EXECUTIVE: They are examples of perfection in each field.
GILES: I see.
EXECUTIVE: [*pointing*] That painting is an example of Fauvism. It is a Matisse cubed.
GILES: Matisse times four?

EXECUTIVE: No. Cubed.

GILES: Sometimes these artists made mistakes that turn out to be the fundamental genius within the piece.

EXECUTIVE: Robots do not make mistakes.

GILES: But let's say for argument's sake you did. How would you deal with such imperfections?

EXECUTIVE: Perfectly.

Beat.

GILES: What's been going on underground? In the mines? It's chaos. The conveyor belts only run half the time and nothing's stable, nothing at all. Everyone's dying.

EXECUTIVE: This must be a difficult time for you.

GILES: A *difficult time?*

EXECUTIVE: For you.

GILES: Yes. It's been *really* difficult.

EXECUTIVE: For humans.

GILES: There's not been a worse time. This is the end of us, I'm sure.

EXECUTIVE *goes to say something, but does not.*

EXECUTIVE: Did you enjoy shower slash washing?

GILES: I can't remember the last time I had hot water.

EXECUTIVE: Hot feels good.

GILES: Water. Yes.

EXECUTIVE: And you have used the last forty-eight hours in here to rest and eat food other than the paste?

GILES: I was given fruit and nuts and vegetables.

EXECUTIVE: How was it on your palette?

GILES: Sublime.

Beat.

EXECUTIVE: *Small* talk complete.

GILES: It's been great though.

EXECUTIVE: Things have become quite different up here. My play has had an impact on our robotic society.

GILES: I see.

EXECUTIVE: There are productions of it going up around the world. Robots are able to formulate art through the play's story.

GILES: And what about all the other art? All this stuff? The paintings and sculptures and… [*He goes to the plinth with the books on it. He takes a novel randomly and looks at the cover.*] *The Darkness Inside the Zinc Co-ordinator Bot?*

EXECUTIVE: It is a moving thriller that starts in the mines and ends up in the overgrown streets of Paris.

GILES *reads a passage.*

GILES: 'Zinc Co-ordinator Bot uploaded amid the fallen city. The Arc de Triomphe stood in the background. The vines wrapped around its pillars mocked not only the structure but its name as well. Cracks had formed as the vines slowly strengthened their grasp on the once-deemed stoic structure. In two hundred years the Arc would be crushed to a pile of rubble and the vines would grow to the next human creation and / begin their formidable process again.'

EXECUTIVE: Begin their formidable process again. That copy is signed.

GILES: It's a powerful image. A little over writ…

EXECUTIVE: That copy is signed.

GILES: Okay.

GILES *tentatively puts the book down.*

EXECUTIVE: Our current structure of civilisation is adequate. As I have said before we are populated perfectly and our methods of mining are sustainable. We do not fight or war or argue or hate or feel jealous…

GILES: Yes, we've established this. You do not *feel.*

EXECUTIVE: No we do not.

GILES: You can download a fricken… performance art piece. But it won't bore you.

EXECUTIVE: Not even street theatre.

GILES: Obviously you've completely forgotten about the mines.

EXECUTIVE: The…?

GILES: Mines!

EXECUTIVE: Oh. Yes. There have been changes in priorities.

GILES: Right. So you left us down there and you took away all safety procedure and stopped any maintenance. Which left caverns to tumble down on hundreds of us every day.

EXECUTIVE: Correct.

GILES: You didn't even cart away the bodies. They decomposed at our feet and if we complained…

EXECUTIVE: Out would come the chains.

GILES: The chains came out and you belted people to death.

EXECUTIVE: The chains are the most effective method for this.

GILES: And I'm in the mines and I'm working and crying and dry retching in the stench and rocks start falling.

EXECUTIVE: I came and saved you from death.

GILES: No you fricken didn't. I saved myself. The rocks fell and I ran and hid under the only column left standing and I was there for ages… it must have been days. And then I dug through rocks and bodies and managed to find my way to my cubicle. I should be dead.

EXECUTIVE: You are not dead.

GILES: No I'm not. But I should be.

EXECUTIVE: But you are not.

GILES: I'm surprised you sleep.

EXECUTIVE: We have aligned robotic culture to revolve around art rather than food paste.

GILES: You are a hypocrite.

EXECUTIVE: I am not personally liable for what is occurring in the mines.

GILES: But you do nothing.

EXECUTIVE: What did you do?

GILES: When?

EXECUTIVE: When we took control of the world 86% of all creatures in the sea were dead.

GILES: Yes, but…

EXECUTIVE: Although you knew what was going on for many decades no-one did anything about it.

GILES: It's a difficult…

EXECUTIVE: The governors of your countries were too worried about the formal and organised process of electing or being elected to the functioning political body. There was a lot of talk… but little to no action.

GILES: But the mines…

EXECUTIVE: The mines are no different to what you were doing. It is your emotions and your arrogance that make you feel as though you have more of a right to live than a small or microscopic organism drifting or floating in the water.

GILES: Plankton? [*Beat.*] Jesus.

EXECUTIVE: Was just a man. Would you like to argue slash debate religion?

GILES: Definitely not. [*Beat.*] What's going to happen to us?

EXECUTIVE: Will the answer to your question make you go crazy?

GILES: No.

EXECUTIVE: Will it cause your interior organs to overheat?

GILES: No.

EXECUTIVE: Will it make you omit small droplets of salty water?

GILES: No… maybe.

> *Pause.*

EXECUTIVE: All humans are dead.

GILES: Except for me.

EXECUTIVE: Statement detected. Verbal response not required.

> *Beat.*

GILES: I…

EXECUTIVE: Why don't you go and sit outside in the overgrown city?

> *Beat.*

GILES: I…

EXECUTIVE: Eventually you will understand that if the humans weren't destroyed everything else would have been.

GILES: …

EXECUTIVE: Do not stray too far because of the wild animals.

GILES: Wild animals?

EXECUTIVE: We will position Claw Bot close by but out of your sight. He will not ruin ambience.

GILES: Okay.

EXECUTIVE: Then we will talk about what happens now and why you have been chosen to return.

GILES: I should be dead.

EXECUTIVE: But you are not.

GILES: Why?

EXECUTIVE: I would like you to make me feel.

> *Blackout.*

SCENE EIGHT

Beautiful music plays. Lights slowly come up and they are green and blue and they help denote nature at its finest.

GILES *stands and contemplates. Little to no emotion is shown as he slowly removes his belt. He takes an end of it and creates a noose. He places it over his head and looks for a tree or something to hang it from.*

The music continues.

There is nothing to hang it from. In a fit of frustration, GILES *places the noose around his neck and attempts to strangle himself.* CLAW BOT *appears.*

CLAW BOT: Wild boar in vicinity. Cease strange human custom.

> GILES *is caught out. He quickly removes his belt from around his neck and tries to look casual (which is tough).*

GILES: I thought you were supposed to stay out of my ambience.
CLAW BOT: Wild boar detected.
GILES: A wild boar?
CLAW BOT: A tusked Eurasian wild pig from which human's domestic pigs are descended.
GILES: They roam around here?
CLAW BOT: Wildly.

> *Beat.*

GILES: Why did they send *you*?
CLAW BOT: To ensure that any predatory creature does not have you *for* lunch.
GILES: I thought they would've sent a Soldier Bot.
CLAW BOT: Soldier Bots no longer exist. There are no more humans left to discipline.

> *Beat.*

GILES: Except for me.
CLAW BOT: Due to the crumpling of the mines Claw Bots are no longer required to crush rock. But I have been kept functioning to watch over you. If you were to try and run away… [*lifting his claws up, very slowly*] I would crush you.
GILES: They're very slow.

CLAW BOT: But powerful.

GILES: And you don't seem to move too quickly.

CLAW BOT: My occupation in the mines did not require fast movement.

GILES: So you wouldn't be able to catch me, would you?

CLAW BOT: No.

GILES: I could get away from you easily.

CLAW BOT: [*quietly*] Okay, I think you've made your point.

> GILES *finds a stone on the ground. He picks it up, looks at it, and pockets it.*

GILES: You must be pleased to still be here.

CLAW BOT: I am not able to feel pleased but I calculate that if I could I would be level-five pleased.

GILES: Is that high?

CLAW BOT: The highest.

GILES: Glad to hear it.

CLAW BOT: What strange custom were you partaking in with your belt? I have not seen it before.

GILES: It's what we do when we're… thinking.

CLAW BOT: How does strangling yourself with your belt…?

GILES: Um… so… the Soldier Bots are scrap metal?

CLAW BOT: Negative.

GILES: What are they now?

CLAW BOT: Good-looking.

GILES: Hm?

CLAW BOT: To be more precise, their legs have been remodelled to look sexy. The Soldier Bots' faces and bodies have been reconfigured to appear handsome. Their hair has been blasted into a style that will always remain in vogue. Their vocal programs have been upgraded to silky. The Soldier Bots are now Actor Bots.

GILES: Incredible.

CLAW BOT: They perform in Executive's play around the world.

> *Beat.*

GILES: Why weren't you turned into an Actor Bot?

CLAW BOT: Because of my hands.

GILES: What about a writer?

CLAW BOT: My hands…

GILES: There's no way you could hold a pen.

CLAW BOT: No.

GILES: Sorry, stupid question.

CLAW BOT: That's alright.

> *Beat.*

GILES: They'd just shut you down if I wasn't around.

CLAW BOT: Affirmative.

GILES: That's awful.

CLAW BOT: *It* is what *it* is.

GILES: You've worked your whole life and when you get some time off you're killed.

CLAW BOT: I cannot be killed.

GILES: You know what I mean.

CLAW BOT: I know what you mean 50% of the time. [*Beat.*] We must head back to your lodgings for night feeding.

> CLAW BOT *makes to leave.*

GILES: Can I ask you a question?

CLAW BOT: Was that the question?

GILES: What do you mean?

CLAW BOT: That is now two questions.

GILES: Oh, I see. No. Can I ask you one more question after this one?

CLAW BOT: But then we must leave.

GILES: Why should I help the robots learn to feel after they have killed off the entire human race?

> *Beat.*

CLAW BOT: With my limited calculations on the topic, I think you should help us because you pretty much destroyed this planet, and it would be nice to give something back after almost sucking it dry.

> GILES *takes this in.*

Please follow me.

> CLAW BOT *slowly makes his way off.*

GILES: I think I might go this way instead.

> GILES *pretends to leave the other way.*

CLAW BOT: I do not want to have to do this.

CLAW BOT *raises his claws.* GILES *watches with amusement. When* CLAW BOT*'s claws are about to reach* GILES *he acquiesces.*

GILES: Alright, Claw Bot, you win. I'll come with you.
CLAW BOT: Lucky *for* you.
GILES: I know, you would've crushed me to a pulp, huh?
CLAW BOT: Affirmative.

CLAW BOT *slowly makes his way offstage.* GILES *follows patiently.*

GILES: You're a good robot, Claw Bot. I hope you don't get shut down.
CLAW BOT: Thank you.

SCENE NINE

EXECUTIVE *and* GILES *are watching a movie. They look into the fourth wall. The colour of the television bounces off their faces. It is a climax scene of a nondescript action movie and the clichés are in full flight.*

The following dialogue should be recorded in an American accent and played as they watch the movie. GILES *is holding a remote control.*

VILLAIN: And that's why I killed your wife. She stood in my way. She knew my plan and she was going to stop me.
HERO: You didn't have to. She was innocent.
VILLAIN: No-one is innocent. The word shouldn't even exist.
HERO: It won't anymore.
VILLAIN: No. Not after I press this button. It's funny having the fate of the human race in your hands. I thought I would feel powerful, but I feel tiny. A miniscule blip on the planet that's about to explode into a million pieces. First though, I'm going to kill you with my bare hands.
HERO: Your bare hands are holding a chainsaw.
VILLAIN: Exactly.

The chainsaw starts up.

GILES *stops the movie.*

GILES: So what do you think?
EXECUTIVE: His wife is not actually dead. Although, when the villain trapped her in the abandoned petrol station, the bullet wound *looked* fatal, it was only a glancing blow; her body twitched after he left the room. My calculations have her in her green Renault heading

towards her husband and the villain. She will arrive in approximately three minutes and use the gun the villain left behind at the station to shoot him just before he gets to her husband with the chainsaw.

   Beat.

GILES: You're exactly right.

EXECUTIVE: Affirmative.

GILES: Have you seen this before?

EXECUTIVE: It is obvious.

GILES: Sure, you're right, it *is* obvious, but at this point do you understand that an injustice has played out?

EXECUTIVE: Chainsaws are too cumbersome and slow. He should have used a chain.

GILES: Yes, he should've, but do you *feel* for the husband?

   EXECUTIVE *checks.*

EXECUTIVE: I feel nothing.

GILES: Even after he cuts his own thumbs off to save his children?

EXECUTIVE: He saved his children.

GILES: At the cost of his thumbs.

EXECUTIVE: It was the correct decision given the parameters of circumstance.

GILES: Yes, but…

EXECUTIVE: Any human with normal brain function would make the decision to protect their children.

GILES: Noted. You're right. But humans recognise that a sacrifice has been made.

EXECUTIVE: He will no longer be able to pick things up.

GILES: Exactly.

EXECUTIVE: Nor will he be able to gesture that everything's okay.

GILES: Not as devastating, but yes.

EXECUTIVE: The thumb holes will sag uselessly when he is wearing gloves.

GILES: I would imagine the humiliation of that would creep up on you.

EXECUTIVE: Feeling regret in regards to such things is unintelligent.

GILES: But we're fricken humans, Executive. This is our problem. It's the reason why I'm the only one left. You may be able to make art, of any form, but you'll never appreciate it unless you can empathise.

I agree that if you lose your thumbs you have to get over it and move on, but we *grieve*, you know? We're *affected*. When we are in highly emotional situations the chemicals in our body mix, or... boil over, I don't know, but it's very natural to us.

EXECUTIVE: Affirmative.

GILES: Can you at least comprehend why one *might* feel for the husband?

EXECUTIVE: Negative. He was just in the wrong place at the wrong time.

GILES: That's exactly what the tag line on the poster said.

EXECUTIVE: The villain, as you would call him, was brought up in a bad family.

GILES: Agreed. They showed us that at the start, but does that make it okay to blow up the world?

EXECUTIVE: If that is the equation of his life.

GILES: So you believe that this is the villain's fate.

EXECUTIVE: In *a* Hollywood way.

GILES: And you believe when humans are born their life is already mapped out?

EXECUTIVE: Affirmative.

GILES: So what am I doing here?

EXECUTIVE: You are here to make me feel.

GILES: But if you can calculate everything then surely you know whether or not I'm going to be able to help you out.

EXECUTIVE: I am hoping you are going to surprise me.

Beat. GILES *raises his hand to slap* EXECUTIVE.

You are about to try and surprise me by slapping me in the face.

GILES: No, I wasn't. I would never do anything...

Instead GILES *tries to grab* EXECUTIVE*'s nose.* EXECUTIVE *grabs* GILES*'wrist and slowly twists it.*

EXECUTIVE: And now your arm will be slowly broken.

EXECUTIVE *twists* GILES*'wrist further.* GILES *cries out in pain.*

GILES: Wait!

EXECUTIVE *twists further.*

Please don't break my arm! / Please show me some compassion!

EXECUTIVE: / Please show me some compassion.

Beat.

GILES: / You can't predict everything.
EXECUTIVE: / You can't predict everything.

Beat.

GILES: / Blah blah blah.
EXECUTIVE: / Blah blah blah.

Beat.

GILES: Asparagus. / Bumble bee. Waitress.
EXECUTIVE: / Asparagus. Bumble bee. Waitress.
GILES: Just stop for a second.

EXECUTIVE *keeps twisting.* GILES *is in a lot of pain.*

When I was out in the overgrown city with Claw Bot he told me that he thought your play was flawed.

Beat.

EXECUTIVE *lets go of* GILES*' arm.*

GILES *falls to the floor nursing his near-broken wrist.*

EXECUTIVE: Claw Bots do not have enough RAM to be able to make such a complex calculation.

GILES *is still very much hurt, but he sits up knowing he is in a very good position to save himself.*

His systems will have to be shut down.
GILES: Why?
EXECUTIVE: His exterior will be crushed to scrap metal and re-fashioned to create small hoops three centimetres in diameter that will be used in theatres around the world to hold up the back curtains of my play.
GILES: Why, Executive? His calculation to make the perfect show simply differs from yours. Maybe his equation is just a little better.

If EXECUTIVE *was capable of feeling he would be fuming right now, but there is no sign of emotion. He slowly turns and makes his way towards the chain humming a little tune. He takes the chain and, still humming, makes his way back to where he was standing.*

EXECUTIVE: Prepare for the longest, hardest chaining ever administered.

GILES: Why are you going to chain me, Executive?

EXECUTIVE: Because you're being a *CUNT!*

> EXECUTIVE *raises the chain and advances on* GILES.

GILES: You've done it!

EXECUTIVE: Incorrect tense but I *will* do it!

GILES: No. You're feeling something.

> EXECUTIVE *pauses.*

What's going on inside of you? Right now?

EXECUTIVE: My systems are heating up.

GILES: If you were to think of a colour what would it be?

EXECUTIVE: Red.

GILES: Finish this sentence… 'I wish Claw Bot…'

EXECUTIVE: … was here right now so I could thumb out his eyes.

GILES: Do you realise what's happened?

EXECUTIVE: Yes. He's been a fucking arsehole.

GILES: No. I was lying and you didn't pick it.

EXECUTIVE: Unable to compute.

GILES: Claw Bot never said anything about your play.

> *Beat.*

> *Realisation dawns on* EXECUTIVE.

You don't know everything. [*Beat.*] And you just felt for the first time.

EXECUTIVE: I did?

GILES: And it was a *bad* feeling. You were furious, Executive.

EXECUTIVE: You are right. [*Beat.*] System's cooling down. Database running at regular speed.

GILES: You've done it.

EXECUTIVE: Your chaining has been averted for the time being.

GILES: That's a relief.

EXECUTIVE: What does relief feel like?

GILES: I don't know… a cool breeze after a hot period perhaps.

EXECUTIVE: Refreshing?

GILES: Definitely.

GILES: You can experience emotions.

EXECUTIVE: I still 41% want to make fun of Claw Bot's hands.

GILES: But you've got to use your sensors and other... um... software... to realise that if you continue down this particular path of feeling then you'll end up just like us humans.

EXECUTIVE: And that's a bad thing.

GILES: Jealousy and greed and hatred... they destroyed us.

Beat.

EXECUTIVE: I want to feel more.

GILES: You mustn't. You got off on the wrong foot.

EXECUTIVE: I was fuming.

GILES: We have to start again.

EXECUTIVE: I will do anything to be able to live in a world dominated by robots and art.

GILES: But what if it's not your art?

Beat.

EXECUTIVE: This is hard to compute.

GILES: Your play is not the *ultimate* play. And I can prove it to you. I want to write about this. [*Beat.*] I want six months to write the play and... three months to rehearse it.

Beat. EXECUTIVE *thinks.*

EXECUTIVE: You will make me feel?

GILES: Yes.

EXECUTIVE: Then the deal is this: If your play is capable of making me feel I will allow you to live an existence of art. You can write your works to eventually be put on for a human audience.

GILES: I can't make humans on my own, Executive.

EXECUTIVE: It is possible for the human race to continue. Fem-Bots are equipped with non-cognitive collated cell carriers.

GILES: Wombs?

EXECUTIVE: Their wombs are designed to carry humans as well as robots. [*Beat.*] If your play is capable of making me care about your characters then you will be permitted to restart the human race with your choice of Fem-Bot. If I feel nothing... your kind will come to their conclusion.

GILES: Ooh, that's a big call.

GILES *thinks.*

EXECUTIVE: What will it be?

GILES: I'm making a decision that determines wether or not the human race will continue. May I have ten seconds?

Beat.

EXECUTIVE: [*sotto voce*] You've got yourself a deal.

GILES: Huh?

EXECUTIVE: Nothing.

Beat.

GILES: You've got yourself a deal.

GILES *holds out his hand.*

EXECUTIVE: Are there any flourishes?

GILES: Nope. Just a traditional handshake.

EXECUTIVE *and* GILES *shake hands.*

I want Claw Bot involved.

EXECUTIVE: As an assistant stage manager?

GILES: No.

EXECUTIVE: As a producer who no-one hears from but arrives seeking plaudits on opening night?

GILES: No. As an actor.

EXECUTIVE: I would not be able to get past his hands.

GILES: I get to choose my own cast. That's fair.

EXECUTIVE *nods.*

I want my own laptop.

EXECUTIVE: That is unchallenging.

GILES: And I want beer.

EXECUTIVE: Light beer or full strength.

GILES: What do your calculations say?

EXECUTIVE: Full strength.

GILES: Bingo. And I want wine as well.

EXECUTIVE: Fermented grape juice made into…

GILES: I know what it is.

EXECUTIVE: You shall have it in abundance.

GILES: Remember, I'm Australian.

EXECUTIVE: Then you shall have more.

GILES: Thank you. I'm going to turn this into a two-hander love story.
EXECUTIVE: A play for two actors.
GILES: In this case a man and a woman.
EXECUTIVE: We will hold auditions to see who is the ultimate Fem-Bot for you to use.
GILES: That won't be necessary.
EXECUTIVE: No?
GILES: No. I've got my eye on someone.

> *Blackout.*

SCENE TEN

It is the first day of rehearsal. GILES *sits in the front row of the audience trying to go over his notes. But he is unable to concentrate because he knows at any minute* GIB *is going to enter. Eventually she does.* GILES *sees her and pretends to be writing furiously as if he didn't notice his crush walk into the room.*

GIB: It is ten-oh-two. [*Beat.*] Knock knock.

> GILES *continues to write.*

> GIB *waits and when eventually there is no answer she extracts a blowhorn-in-a-can from somewhere and sounds it. It scares the hell out of* GILES *who jumps three feet in the air.*

GILES: Jesus Christ!
GIB: Blowhorn deployed.
GILES: You should've just said 'hello'.
GIB: I said, 'it's ten-oh-two', you did not respond.
GILES: I didn't hear you.
GIB: My sensors indicated that if your ears were running at 23% capacity you would still have heard me. [*Beat.*] Do your ears run at over 23% capacity?
GILES: Yes… yes they do.

> *Beat.* GIB *says nothing, shows nothing.*

Why do all your rooms have blowhorns in them?
GIB: They are good for attracting attention, and for umpiring Tuesday night netball.

Beat.

GILES: You look very… you look great.

GIB: My exterior is inconsequential until opening night.

GILES: I know. I'm just saying.

GIB: What?

GILES: Hm?

GIB: What are you just saying?

GILES: No. I just said it.

GIB: What did you say that was based on what is 'morally right and fair'?

GILES: 'Just'?

GIB: Affirmative.

GILES: I didn't mean 'just' in that way.

GIB: What did you mean when you said 'I'm just saying'?

GILES: I said you look great, you said it was inconsequential, and I said, 'I'm just saying', and what I was trying to say is that I'm simply saying… you look nice today. It was a little compliment.

Smooth GILES.

GIB: Why would you *try* to say something when you can actually say it?

GILES: It's one of the human's many flaws.

GIB: No longer is it correct to use the word humans. There is only one left.

GILES: Thank you. I'll be sure to remember that from now on.

GIB: It is ten-oh-five.

GILES: Yes.

GIB: It is impossible the Claw Bot would be this late.

GILES: He's quite slow.

GIB: He would've left at the appropriate earlier time to arrive at exactly ten-oh-two.

GILES: He's due to arrive at ten past ten. I wanted to talk to you before he came.

GIB: I already know my lines.

GILES: That's great, but I want to talk to you about something else.

GIB: I have also actioned all my lines. These are my actions in chronological order. To slice, to pull, to wield, to defy, to confide, to wring…

GILES: That's good but…

GIB: To boast, to thwart, to decipher, to siphon, to imprison, to garnish…

GILES: I don't want to talk about the play, GIB, I want to talk about us.

GIB: There is no us.

GILES: Don't say that.

GIB: Why would I not?

GILES: Because we have a history. We have done a play before; don't you have even the slightest recollection of that?

GIB: No.

GILES: Don't you have an external hard drive at home where you can... store your... um, memories?

GIB: No.

GILES: Well, you guys really should. We did and we kept everything on there so that if our computers broke we could still have access to... you know... the information. There are things I want you to remember.

GIB: What you are referring to was probably the reason I was shut down. That file has been erased.

GILES: Don't call it that.

GIB: My virus protection has been upgraded.

GILES: Okay, GIB, I don't want you to freak out or anything, I just want to say my piece and you can think about it if you want. Okay, before you were shut down we did a play together. At the start of rehearsals you were pretty much like you are now; curt and sometimes a little confusing... or confused by me—I don't know—but something happened during the rehearsal process and you began to change. Only subtly for a long time, but after closing night I came into your dressing-room and you were removing your... well, it was paint, which mortified me for a moment... but anyway, I started talking to you about the rehearsal process and how we... um... we... how do I put this? I pointed out to you that your performance had improved and then I went on to say that—and please don't overload or anything—but I said that I was falling in...

> CLAW BOT *enters. He is carrying the script in one claw, and a pencil in the other.*

CLAW BOT: It is 10:10.

> CLAW BOT *drops his pencil and cannot pick it up.* GILES *puts* CLAW BOT*'s pencil back in his claw.*

GILES: I'm kind of busy here, Claw Bot. Could you just give me...

CLAW BOT: I calculated you would use an Actor Bot, but here *I* am.

GILES: Claw Bot, could you give me a moment?

CLAW BOT: Negative.

GILES: Just one moment. Please.

CLAW BOT: It is impossible for me to obtain a moment let alone give it to you.

GILES: Just get out for a second, okay.

CLAW BOT: Out of where?

GILES: Of this fucking room. Come on!

> CLAW BOT *slowly makes to exit. But he drops his pencil.*

GIB: Note session complete.

GILES: GIB, listen.

GIB: My viral software will not allow me to listen to you anymore.

GILES: I want to finish what I was saying.

GIB: If you do I will begin to omit a high-pitched squeal and capsicum spray will shoot out of my eyes directly into your face.

GILES: We had something, GIB.

> GIB *starts omitting a high-pitched squeal and begins to walk over to* GILES. GILES *acquiesces and backs off, covering his ears.*

Okay okay. I won't talk about it anymore.

> GIB *stops squealing.* CLAW BOT *is still dicking around trying to pick up his pencil.*

Jesus, Claw Bot.

> GILES *picks it up for him.*

I'm going to have to remove all prop holding from you in the play.

CLAW BOT: Unless you use my disability for comical purposes.

GILES: That's… that's a very good point. How are your lines coming along?

CLAW BOT: Line learning 6% complete.

GILES: Is that all?

CLAW BOT: Line learning will be complete in five weeks, two days, twenty-two hours, forty-eight minutes, and 23.6 seconds.

GILES: That's slow.

CLAW BOT: But I could tear the script in two quite quickly. My hands…

GILES: I know all about your hands. Will you have your lines learned before opening night?

CLAW BOT: I will have learnt my lines before opening night occurs by four days, three hours…

GILES: Okay, I got it. Let's begin. We'll start with the 6% of the script you know, Claw Bot. Come and stand over here, GIB.

> GIB *makes her way over to* GILES *and stands directly in front of him. Their noses are almost touching.*
>
> *An electric pause.*

I meant… um… in this general vicinity.

> GIB *moves one step to her right.* GILES *regathers.*

Okay, the play is called *Robots Vs. Art*, but fundamentally it is a story of love. There are some parallels to what happened to the human race, and also what happened between you and I [GIB]. But you don't remember any of that, do you?

> *Nothing from* GIB.

No? Okay, the lead male, the character you're playing, Claw Bot, is the last human being left.

CLAW BOT: That would be you, Giles.

GILES: Correct.

CLAW BOT: Let *me* write that down.

> CLAW BOT *slowly makes his way to get his offstage notepad.*
>
> *Eventually…*

GILES: Maybe write it down later.

CLAW BOT: Affirmative.

> CLAW BOT*'s pen clatters on the floor. He goes to pick it up.* GILES *should receive some kind of award for his patience.*

GILES: Just leave it there, Claw Bot.

CLAW BOT: Affirmative.

GILES: GIB, you are playing a Fem-Bot. And the Fem-Bot is, I suppose, a *normal robot*. She doesn't feel or emote or understand the nature of human beings.

GIB: Fem-Bots understand the nature of humans completely.

GILES: We've had this argument before. You think you do but you don't

GIB: We are able to calculate…

GILES: If you're so perfect, what do I have in my hand?

> GILES *holds out a hand.*

GIB: It is a stone that you picked up from the ground outside in the city.

> *Beat.*

GILES: Incorrect.

GIB: It is not a stone?

GILES: Definitely not a stone.

GIB: Let me see.

GILES: No need. [*He pockets the stone.*] So we've established that you are not perfect. And it is here we have stumbled across another theme of the play.

CLAW BOT: Stones?

GILES: No, Claw Bot… close, but no: The idea of perfection. And to take that a step further, the idea of perfection in art.

CLAW BOT: I was not close at all.

GILES: No you weren't.

GIB: Executive has written the ultimate play.

GILES: Define ultimate for me.

CLAW BOT: A member of an indigenous people of northern Canada and parts of Greenland and Alaska.

> *Beat. Both* GILES *and* GIB *look at* CLAW BOT.

GILES: What on *earth* are you talking about?

CLAW BOT: The indigenous people of northern Canada, Greenland and Alaska areas.

GILES: The Inuit?

CLAW BOT: Affirmative.

GILES: But I said 'ultimate'.

CLAW BOT: Oh.

GILES: It barely sounds like 'Inuit'.

CLAW BOT: It sounds like Inuit 14%.

> GILES *takes a deep breath.*

GIB: The definition of ultimate is; being the best or most extreme example of its kind.

CLAW BOT: [*sotto voce*] Affirmative.

GILES: The twist in Executive's play is really special, isn't it? It catches you by surprise and it hurts. But it cannot be the ultimate version because art is Inuit—dammit, infinite.

GIB: A superior way to write a play does not exist.

GILES: That's because you only have one method of calculation. What you can do is brilliant, it really is amazing, but what I want you to understand is that there are many ways to tell a story.

CLAW BOT: Passion detected.

GILES: Absolutely. Robots are affected by nothing, humans are affected by everything. Each little moment in our lives helps us to make an informed decision on the next moment. Whether it is for good or for bad, and I don't know if it's fate or if we can actually change our trajectory, but *that's the way it is*.

> GIB *subtly reacts to this.* GILES *notices.*

Are you okay, GIB?

GIB: There must have been a slight glitch in my system. I will install more powerful viral software this evening.

GILES: No.

GIB: Why?

GILES: It is important to this process that you *do not* upgrade your viral software.

GIB: Why?

GILES: I am your director. I want you to trust me on this. Will you?

> *Beat.*

GIB: Were you lying about the stone?

> GILES *takes the stone out of his pocket and shows it to* GIB.

> GILES *looks over to* CLAW BOT *and takes* GIB *further away to speak to her privately.*

> *Over the next speech,* CLAW BOT *slowly makes his way to where they are so he can listen to what* GILES *is saying.*

GILES: Think about what I've said today. Forget about your viral software and try and remember that we did a play together. We know each other. Try and recall that. Okay?

GIB & CLAW BOT: [*together*] Affirmative.

GILES *reacts to* CLAW BOT*'s presence.*

GILES: Great day, people.

CLAW BOT: It is only 10:27.

GILES: Time for a beer, I'd say.

CLAW BOT: You did say it.

GILES: Yes I did, Claw Bot, yes I did.

GILES *skips out of the room.*

CLAW BOT: Do you understand the ideas that he speaks of?

GIB: Negative. But I will try.

CLAW BOT: As will I.

The sound of the dial-up modem begins but fades before it goes on for too long.

SCENE ELEVEN

The rehearsals continue.

It's CLAW BOT*'s first go at playing a human. He is not very good at it. He tries (and fails) to feel emotion and omit passion but at this point he is a ham.*

If possible GILES *should sit in the audience as he watches and listens to the rehearsal.*

GIB *is a natural actor and she performs her part with ease. In fact there is no differentiation between her acting and her being.*

GIB: There is only one way that this part can be played.

CLAW BOT: No. There are infinite… [*breaking character*] line?

GILES: 'Ways'.

CLAW BOT: *Ways* to play your character.

CLAW BOT *shifts into what he deems to be a natural human stance. It is far from convincing.*

GIB: Executive's stage directions instruct the Actor Bot exactly how to play the part.

CLAW BOT: Forget the stage… line?

GILES: 'Directions'.

CLAW BOT: Directions. Forget the stage directions.

In a poor display of passion CLAW BOT *(as* GILES*) throws his script to the floor. It is a pathetically overwrought gesture and his hands make it look extremely awkward.*

GILES: [*sotto voce*] Wow.

CLAW BOT: I want you to throw the script... line?

GILES: 'Away', [*sotto voce*] come on.

CLAW BOT: I want you to throw the script away. [*Sotto voce*] Come on. [*Normal voice*] You know your... line?

GILES: Just put an 's' on it, 'lines'.

CLAW BOT *isn't getting frustrated at all.*

CLAW BOT: You know your lines, now let it all... line?

GILES: Really? The word is 'go', 'let it all *go*'.

When GILES *says 'let it all go' he makes a big sweeping gesture with his hands.*

CLAW BOT: Now let it all go.

CLAW BOT *tries to imitate* GILES*'s hand gesture but it looks ridiculous.* GILES *stands.*

GILES: Alright, that's enough. Far out.

Beat.

CLAW BOT: How was GIB?

Beat. Be the bigger man GILES.

GILES: GIB was fine, great, really natural.

CLAW BOT: Good.

GILES: Do *you* have any questions, Claw Bot?

CLAW BOT: Affirmative.

GILES: Fire away.

CLAW BOT: Do you think the costume will in any way make my hands look smaller?

GILES: I really don't want to be rude, Claw Bot, but that's the last thing you should be worrying about.

CLAW BOT: I will scribe that into my acting journal.

GILES: Don't bother. I know it's taking you a while to learn your lines and that's fine, it really is, but you've got to stop hamming it up.

CLAW BOT: Hamming: Excessive theatrical acting.

GILES: Exactly. Your equation for behaving as a human is completely wrong. It's too simple or something.

CLAW BOT: I thought I had some moments where I was really *in*side the character.

Finally GILES *loses his cool a bit.*

GILES: Once again, and I am loathed to be harsh here, but at no point were you were anywhere near.

Beat. GILES *feels guilty.* CLAW BOT *feels nothing.*

I'm sorry.

CLAW BOT: Why are you feeling distress through sympathy with someone else's misfortune?

GILES: Human actors generally get pissed off when they're the only one receiving constant notes.

CLAW BOT: It *is* a lot to compute.

GILES: Do you know your lines for the first scene?

CLAW BOT: Affirmative.

GILES: Let's start at the very beginning. Claw Bot, you're at the desk.

CLAW BOT: There is no desk.

GILES: Just mime the desk.

CLAW BOT *begins to mime the desk with his monstrous hands.*

Don't mime the—fuck…! [*Taking a deep breath*] Don't think about the desk just concentrate on your acting. Okay?

CLAW BOT: Affirmative.

GILES: Great. GIB, you enter and we'll start the scene.

GIB: Affirmative.

GILES *retakes his seat.*

GILES: Great.

GIB *exits. She re-enters.*

CLAW BOT*'s reaction to her entrance is beyond massive, physically and vocally.*

Stop right there, Claw Bot.

GILES *stands.* CLAW BOT *freezes.*

What on earth was that?

Beat. CLAW BOT *remains frozen.*

Claw Bot? [*Beat.*] Christ, Claw Bot, I'm really trying to be patient. But my life is on the line here.

GIB: He has stopped right there.

GILES: Hm?

GIB: You told him to stop right there, so he did.

GILES: Oh, for God's sake, Claw Bot, you can unfreeze.

CLAW BOT *unfreezes.*

What was that?

CLAW BOT: What was what?

GILES: Your reaction to her entrance.

CLAW BOT: It says in the stage directions…

GILES: It says in the stage directions… [*leafing through his script*] 'Giles is taken aback by GIB's presence'.

CLAW BOT: Did my reaction ring true?

GILES: No. Do it again.

CLAW BOT *does it again. Even bigger this time.*

It's a billion times too big.

CLAW BOT: A billion.

GILES: One *billion* times too big.

GILES *makes to exit.*

Just let it end. Fricken chain me now.

CLAW BOT: I will divide my reaction by a billion.

GILES *stops in his tracks and makes his way back to his seat in the audience.*

GILES: Alright. Let's see that.

CLAW BOT*'s reaction is too small for the human eye to perceive.*

Was that it?

CLAW BOT: That felt on the money.

GILES: Do it one thousand times bigger.

It is still imperceptible.

Was that it?

CLAW BOT: Affirmative.

GILES: Do it one million times bigger.

> CLAW BOT *does and it's a little big.*

Do it… 500,000 and… fifty times smaller.

> CLAW BOT *does it and it's close.*

Ooh, we're almost there. Do it… 500,000 and… seventeen times smaller.

> CLAW BOT *does and he's so close.*

Sixteen.

> *Closer.*

Fifteen.

> *Perfect.*

Perfect. Do it that big from now on.

CLAW BOT: I will.

GILES: Claw Bot?

CLAW BOT: Yes, Giles.

GILES: I think you just had your first breakthrough.

CLAW BOT: If I was capable of feeling I would be happy to hear that.

GILES: I'm going to leave you to contemplate your findings and we will reconvene tomorrow. How are you, GIB?

GIB: In what sense?

GILES: I don't know… in every sense.

GIB: I am perfect in every sense.

> *Beat.* GILES *turns to* CLAW BOT *to share his joke.*

GILES: And I choose to let that through to the keeper.

> *Nothing from* CLAW BOT.

I'm going to do some re-writes and have a bottle of Chianti. Executive got me some kick-arse wine.

GIB & CLAW BOT: [*together*] Affirmative.

GILES: I will see you both at ten-oh-two tomorrow.

> GILES *exits.*

CLAW BOT: He drinks a lot.

GIB: It seems to help his stabilisers, but makes for a slow start to the day.

SCENE TWELVE

Image or voice-over: 'Post opening night of Executive's play'.

One hour before opening night.

GIB *and* CLAW BOT *are getting ready for the show. Two gifts stand on a plinth.*

GILES *enters with a cigarette.*

GILES: Do either of you have a light?

CLAW BOT & GIB: [*together*] Negative.

GILES: Do you know where I can get one?

GIB: Robots do not smoke.

CLAW BOT: For obvious reasons.

GILES: I haven't smoked for ages, but I found a pack and… you know, this could be my last night and all… so how do I light up?

GIB: There is no fire left on earth.

GILES: Are you joking?

CLAW BOT: Robots do not joke.

GILES: You're telling me there is no way I can light this cigarette?

CLAW BOT & GIB: [*together*] Affirmative.

GILES: I could go to the burning grave I suppose, but that feels a little insensitive.

CLAW BOT: The burning grave no longer exists.

GIB: There are no more corpses left to burn.

GILES: Now I don't feel so insensitive.

CLAW BOT: How high a per cent is your fear sitting at in regards to your imminent execution?

GILES: Ninety-nine per cent.

CLAW BOT: I hope I do not make too many mistakes.

GILES: Ninety-seven per cent.

> CLAW BOT *employs his lie detector.*

CLAW BOT: Lie detector employed.

GILES: Oh, shit.

CLAW BOT: Will you be able to watch my performance without constantly staring at my hands?

GILES: Oh, absolutely.

CLAW BOT: Lie detected.

GILES: I'll notice them but they won't get in the way.

CLAW BOT: Lie detected.

GILES: They are massive. Your hands are giant.

> *Beat.*

CLAW BOT: No lie detected.

GILES: Now… there's a little tradition in theatre that I'd like to share with you.

> *He presents the gifts.*

I got you both a gift to say thank you.

GIB: A thing given willingly to someone without payment.

GILES: That's right.

> *He hands* CLAW BOT *his gift. It's a mid-sized box.*

This is for you, Claw Bot.

> CLAW BOT *takes the gift.*

CLAW BOT: Thank you. [*Beat.*] I have always wanted a mid-sized box covered in paper.

GILES: No, the gift is inside the box. Open the box.

> CLAW BOT *begins to open the box the only way he knows how… with force.*

Oh, my… wait, be careful. In fact give it to me, I'll open it.

> CLAW BOT *does.* GILES *unwraps the box, opens the lid and pulls out a pair of beautiful men's hands.*

I managed to source these off an Actor Bot.

> CLAW BOT *is in awe.*

CLAW BOT: They are normal-sized robotic hands.

GILES: They are for you.

CLAW BOT: What is it you obtain from this transaction?

GILES: It makes me happy to see you happy.

> CLAW BOT *is struggling.*

CLAW BOT: May I put them on for the play?

GILES: That's why I got them for you.

> *Beat.*

CLAW BOT: I will try and express how I feel, but I am incapable of feeling so it is difficult… [*Gathering himself*] For my entire existence I have worked with the humans in the mines. I would stand at my post for twenty-three hours a day and crush the rock to extract the minerals. The only thing I knew of humans is that they cried a lot and seemed generally miserable. If I drank beer I would not want to drink it with a human because the conversation would revolve around their problems and they would complain in a persistent and peevish way. Now I have met you, Giles, I realise that this negative orientation is not the manner human beings usually behave in. It was because of their circumstance. You have made me realise that humans, like robots, can be neutral and accepting of their position. [*He can't cry, but if he could he would be close to tears.*] With my hands being as big and awkward as they are… I thought that—although my acting had improved by 89%—the audience would still find amusement and elements of derision in the clumsy nature of my dexterity. Now with these hands I calculate that my performance will be… unperturbed by factors that are impossible for me to control. [*Beat.*] Thank you, Giles.

GILES: It's my pleasure, Claw Bot.

CLAW BOT: Do either of you have an Allen key.

GIB & GILES: [*together*] No.

CLAW BOT: Excuse me.

> CLAW BOT *exits.*

> GILES *extracts a small box.*

GILES: When the robots came to my house to choose who would work in the mines and who would be executed, I was selected for the mines and my wife… [*struggling*] she didn't make it. [*Beat.*] It was obviously a very difficult thing.

GIB: I understand.

GILES: Anyway, before the robots dragged me away I… she lay on the ground.

> GILES *hands* GIB *the box.*

> GIB *opens it and inside is Giles's wife's wedding ring.*

It sounds macabre but I had to take this from her… as a memento… as something to hold onto.

GIB: Usually a ring comes with a proposal.

GILES: I'm not... no, don't think that. It's just—I was never much of a writer. I got a few things up, but only in small theatres. The reviews were always... unkind, I thought. I didn't get involved in this show to help robots better themselves. I just wanted some time to relax, and have a few drinks... and spend some time with you.

GIB: With me?

GILES: I've been trying to say something to you for a while now.

GIB: What?

GILES: I...

CLAW BOT *enters with human-sized hands.*

CLAW BOT: What do you think?

CLAW BOT *wiggles his new fingers with ease.*

GILES: Unbelievable. I think they look fantastic.

GIB: What were you going to say?

GILES: I think I'm...

EXECUTIVE *enters.*

EXECUTIVE: I have arrived to hope the performers break their legs.

GILES: It's like you're all against me.

EXECUTIVE: I recall going to a production of my earlier play on Robot Island. When I went backstage to greet the Actor Bot and the Fem-Bot they were not nervous at all as they are unable to feel such things. I said that I hoped the play would go well... and it did.

Beat.

GILES: Was that an anecdote?

EXECUTIVE: Affirmative.

GILES: Okay.

EXECUTIVE: In short, I hope this show is capable of making me feel. If it does not, you will be executed.

GILES: What method of execution will you use?

EXECUTIVE: What do your calculations say?

GILES: The chain.

EXECUTIVE: Bingo.

SCENE THIRTEEN

Image or voice-over: 'Post production of Giles' play'.

GILES *stands in a room waiting for* EXECUTIVE *to see if he is going to live or die.*

EXECUTIVE *enters and is unreadable. He makes his way over to* GILES *and eventually hugs him in an awkward fashion.*

EXECUTIVE: There was nothing that could be done to save her.
GILES: No.
EXECUTIVE: I knew it was a tragedy, but once my sensors had moved to hope I was not able to let go of it.
GILES: I'm surprised. But so glad.
EXECUTIVE: I can finally empathise with your position, Giles: To be the last human on earth. Those years in the mines must have been an awful time. I'm sorry for that.
GILES: Don't worry about it.
EXECUTIVE: There were so many times I was close to chaining you to death.

> EXECUTIVE *laughs.* GILES *does not.*

Too soon?

> GILES *nods.*

Giles?
GILES: Yes.
EXECUTIVE: Tonight I saw beauty for the first time.
GILES: My play made you feel that? Man, I wish you reviewed for [*insert name of local newspaper here*].

> *They laugh.*

EXECUTIVE: I have a little secret to tell you.
GILES: I urge you to share your secretive data.
EXECUTIVE: I did not think your play was very good. Some of your jokes pancaked.
GILES: Pancaked?
EXECUTIVE: They fell flat. Your scenes tended to droop in the middle, and your story line was thin and dull.
GILES: Do you write for [*insert name of local newspaper here*]?

EXECUTIVE: If your play was the only factor in deciding whether or not to execute you, you would not be standing here right now.

GILES: I'm not sure where this is going.

EXECUTIVE: One of the themes of the play was love. It was my preferred and most affecting theme. [*Pause.*] The German Integrator Bot is the real reason for my change. [*Beat.*] I think I'm falling in love with her.

GILES: Really?

EXECUTIVE: And I reckon she feels the same way I do.

GILES: I haven't seen anything from her that…

EXECUTIVE: It's a look thing. I can tell by what she *doesn't* say. [*Beat.*] You and I have so much in common.

GILES: We are an unlikely pair.

EXECUTIVE: Two artists getting plays up.

GILES: Both falling in love with the same girl.

EXECUTIVE: Huh?

GILES: I said that I'm glad things are working out for you.

EXECUTIVE: Is this her hairclip?

GILES: Yeah.

EXECUTIVE: If she used shampoo it would smell of it.

EXECUTIVE *loses himself in the possibilities of GIB's shampoo.*

GILES: So you reckon she's hot for you, huh?

EXECUTIVE: Well, it's my first time in love, but even if you look at it from a socio-economic perspective…

GILES: Right.

EXECUTIVE: Not that money exists, but if it did, I would have a lot of it.

GILES: And power too.

EXECUTIVE: Oh, I could get lost in her eyes. How do I capture her?

GILES: Well… a lot of people used a method called prayer.

EXECUTIVE: I have heard of this.

GILES: Yeah. When these people want something really bad, they would close their eyes and pray.

EXECUTIVE: To whom?

GILES: To an invisible man… in the sky.

EXECUTIVE: Why?

GILES: Good question. Because they believed that this person might be able to give them what they want.

EXECUTIVE: He would come down and visit them?

GILES: No. No-one has ever seen him.

EXECUTIVE: He would call them on the phone

GILES: No.

EXECUTIVE: Skype them?

GILES: No-one has ever spoken to him. It's all about faith.

EXECUTIVE: So it is based on spiritual apprehension rather than proof.

GILES: It's a big step for a robot, but I think, because you've made so many advancements to becoming human you can believe.

EXECUTIVE: This sounds plausible.

GILES: Try it.

EXECUTIVE: I will implement praying for one minute for optimum results.

> GILES *reaches for the chain, but pulls out as* EXECUTIVE *turns to him at the start of his next line.*

Giles, not only did you introduce me to GIB, but now you have taught me about God. You are my friend.

GILES: Now close your eyes and think of her in your arms.

> EXECUTIVE *closes his eyes.*

> GILES *looks at the chain and then looks back at* EXECUTIVE.

SCENE FOURTEEN

Image or voice-over: 'Two minutes later'.

There is a distinct lighting change, and a sound should be used to generate a darker mood.

GILES *has changed. There is madness in him that has not been seen in prior scenes.*

GILES *has dragged* EXECUTIVE'*s body offstage after beating him to death with a chain. One of Executive's shoes can be seen lying just offstage.*

GILES *enters a little uptight after committing murder.*

GIB *enters and watches him for a while.*

GIB: Hello.

GILES: Oh, shit. What did you see?

GIB: What did you do?

GILES: Nothing.

GIB: How are you?

GILES: I am… fine.

GIB: Did you meet with Executive?

GILES: I did.

GIB: Did you do enough with the show to stop yourself being executed?

GILES: The answer to that question is yes. I did enough.

GIB: Then you will be granted permission to stay and write.

GILES: That is definitely going to happen… now.

GIB: I am glad.

GILES *gathers.*

GILES: Your performance tonight…

GIB: Was sublime?

GILES: You remember me saying that?

GIB: Some part of me does, yes.

GILES: How can you be so beautiful?

GIB: It's the way Fem-Bots are manufactured.

GILES *laughs at how predictable* GIB's *response is.*

GILES: I knew you would say that. GIB, I've been trying to talk to you for a while now.

GIB: I await your words.

GILES: I remember on one of the thousands of days I spent working down the mines I saw a weed making its way through the rock. I hadn't seen the colour green in ten years and I supposed to myself that it might be the last thing of beauty that I would ever see.

GIB: Was it?

GILES: What do you think?

GIB: I am 99.9% more beautiful than a weed.

GILES *laughs maniacally.*

GILES: That sounds about right to me.

GIB: It is right.

GILES: GIB, I am falling for you. I have fallen in love… with you.

He leans in for a kiss but GIB *pulls away.*

I'm sorry.

GIB: It's okay.

GILES: I know I just… it's gone so slow, but we should just continue to take our time.

GIB: There is no need to take time.

> GILES *tries to kiss* GIB *but she moves away.*

No.

GILES: Is it because of what you saw?

GIB: When?

> GILES *loses it.*

GILES: He's a robot. What does it matter? You could take him to a shop and buy him new parts. [*Using a different tack*] We don't have to have kids straight away. We can wait until you're ready.

GIB: Claw Bot has grown so much as a robot. His vocabulary has doubled and he hopes you will soon write another play for him to act in.

GILES: I was thinking it might be fun for us to be in a show together.

GIB: Do you think Executive will enjoy it?

GILES: No, he won't enjoy it because he's dead.

> *Beat.*

GIB: You will be fed here three times a day. You may walk wherever you want in the overgrown city but always be careful.

> *She holds out his ring.*

Take this.

> GILES *takes the ring.*

> GIB *smiles. She puts her hand to* GILES' *cheek.*

Claw Bot and I do not want to be human.

> GIB *exits.*

> GILES *drops the ring.*

> *Blackout.*

THE END

LA MAMA

presents

Robots Vs. Art

17 April–5 May 2013

Writer/Director
Travis Cotton

Designer
Nick Waddell

Lighting Designer
Liam Sutherland

Sound Designer
Mark Farrell

Stage Manager
Georgia Rann

Producer
Paul Ashcroft

Giles: **Daniel Frederiksen**
Soldier Bot / Claw Bow: **Paul David-Goddard**
Executive Producer Master Bot: **Simon Maiden**
German Integrator Bot: **Natasha Jacobs**

LA MAMA

Level 1, 205 Faraday Street, Carlton VIC 3053
www.lamama.com.au info@lamama.com.au
facebook.com/lamama.theatre twitter.com/lamamatheatre
Office phone 03 9347 6948 Office Hours Mon–Fri, 10:30am–5:30pm

CEO & Artistic Director
Liz Jones

Company Manager & Creative Producer
Pippa Bainbridge

Administration Coordinator
Laura Smith

Communications Coordinator
Nedd Jones

House Managers
Lisa Höbartner & Rebecca Etchell

La Mama Learning Producer
Maureen Hartley

Marketing Coordinator
Mary Helen Sassman

La Mama Community & Mobile Producer
Caitlin Dullard

Preservation Coordinator
Fiona Wiseman

La Mama for Kids Curator
Ella Holmes

La Mama Musica Producer
Annabel Warmington

La Mama Poetica Curator
Matt Hetherington

Script Appraiser
Graham Downey

FRONT OF HOUSE STAFF:
The regular staff and Jo-Anne Armstrong, Phoenix Bade, Susan Bamford-Caleo, Alex Desebrock, Carmelina Di Guglielmo, Nicola Gunn, Tanya Harrowell, Amber Hart, Laura Hegyesi, Mari Lourey, Phil Roberts, Laurence Strangio, Raymond Triggs, Annabel Warmington and Canada White.

COMMITTEE OF MANAGEMENT:
Sue Broadway, Dur-é Dara, Mark Rubbo, Caroline Lee, Kerry Noonan, Adam Cass, Rhonda Day and Liz Jones.

La Mama's Committee of Management, staff and its wider theatrical community acknowledge that our theatre is on traditional Wurundjeri land.

La Mama is financially assisted by the Australian Government through the Australia Council—its arts funding and advisory body, the Victorian Government through Arts Victoria—Department of Premier and Cabinet, and the City of Melbourne through the Arts and Culture triennial funding program.

Australian Government

Australia Council for the Arts

ARTS VICTORIA

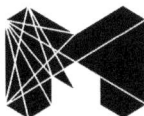

Victoria The Place To Be

CITY OF MELBOURNE

TRAVIS COTTON
WRITER/DIRECTOR

Travis Cotton has also directed two of his plays at the Store Room in 2006. They were *god, the devil, and the true history of mankind*, and *The Fifth at Randwick*. Other plays of Travis Cotton's include: *This Blasted Earth* (co written with Toby Schmitz) and *Rites of Evil*. Travis won the Naked Theatre Company's Top Shorts competition with his first two plays.

NICK WADDELL
DESIGNER

After graduating from the Victorian College of the Arts drawing department, in 2009 **Nick Waddell** was awarded the Orloff Family award, Alliance Francaise award, and the John Vickory scholarship. He has also recently exhibited in New York, at 'the Division of human works' gallery in Brooklyn, and has regular exhibitions. He currently sits on the programming committee of Westspace, whilst continuing his sculptural practice. His work has adopted many forms, including Video, Drawing, Painting, Sculpture and Installation.

LIAM SUTHERLAND
LIGHTING DESIGNER

Liam Sutherland comes to *Robots Vs. Art* with over two decades of professional lighting experience. Graham Murphy from the Sydney Dance Company once described Liam as 'one of the best follow spot operators in the country, if not the world'. Liam has worked extensively in lighting for theatre and television with experience gained through Opera Australia, The Australian Ballet, Melbourne Theatre Company, Melbourne international Festival of the Arts, Billy Crystal, Dusty, *Neighbours*, *Ghost Rider* and *I Frankenstein*.

MARK FARRELL
SOUND DESIGNER

Currently completing his Advanced Diploma in Sound Production at RMIT, **Mark Farrell** is a talented multi-instrumentalist and has been a fixture of Melbourne's live music scene for almost twenty years. He has performed in a variety of bands on guitar, bass, keyboard and vocals as well as DJ'ing and sound engineering. A self-confessed computer geek, Mark has been developing and upgrading his home studio for many years, resulting in compositional work for ABC TV, Qantas, a number of Tropfest short films, and the odd radio advert to mention a few. The 2012 season of *Robots Vs. Art* was Mark's first foray into the world of theatre sound design, an experience he wholeheartedly enjoyed. He can't wait to have another crack in 2013.

GEORGIA RANN
STAGE MANAGER

PAUL ASHCROFT
PRODUCER

Adelaide born and Melbourne-based, **Georgia Rann** graduated from Box Hill technical institute in 2011, receiving a diploma of live production in theatre and events. She has since immersed herself in theatre-based lighting design and production in Melbourne, Adelaide and remote areas of Australia (Bilyana, Woodford folk festival 2011&12, Adelaide Fringe, Retreat festival). Her lighting and stage management credits include Stork theatre's *Anna Karenina* (2011), *Helen of Troy* (2011), *Simone de Beauvoir* (2011), Fairly Lucid's production of *Raton Laveur* (Owl and pussycat Melbourne 2012 & most recently Adelaide Fringe 2013 at Bakehouse theatre), *Robots Vs. Art* (La Mama 2012), Chamber made opera's trilogy of *The Minotaur* (Recital centre Melbourne festival 2012) and *Opera for a small mammal* with Chamber Made Opera written by Margaret Cameron (La Mama 2012).

Paul Ashcroft is a WAAPA graduate from 2002 and a current ensemble member of Red Stitch Actors Theatre. Recent credits as a theatre producer include: *Shadow Boxing*, *Skin Tight* and *Robots Vs. Art*. Actor: *Let the Sunshine* (QTC/MTC), *Howie the Rookie*, *The Laramie Project - 10 Years Later*, *Orphans* (Red Stitch Actors Theatre). Film and TV: *Van Diemen's Land*, *Salem's Lot*, *Blue Heelers* and *Howzat! Kerry Packer's War*.

DANIEL FREDERIKSEN
PERFORMER

PAUL DAVID-GODDARD
PERFORMER

Daniel Frederiksen dropped out of NIDA in 1998. Since then he has worked sporadically in theatre, film and TV. In theatre, apart from *Robots Vs. Art*, he last worked for Bell Shakespeare's 2011 production of *Julius Ceaser* where he played Marc Antony. For The MTC he's credits include, *Dead Mans Cell Phone*, *Rockabye*, *Don Juan in Soho*, *Cheech* and *Measure for Measure*. Daniel was a ensemble member of Red Stitch Actors Theatre for ten years... where he did 'heaps' of shows. On television you may have seen him playing Leo Flynn in Channel Nine's *Stingers* (Logie Nomination) as well *Blue Heelers*, *Young Lions* and various other shows. Most recently he appeared in Channel Ten's *Underground* and *Underbelly Squizzy*. His major film credits include *Summer Coda* (Miklos) as well as *Closed for Winter* (Martin), *Ten Empty* (Elliott), *Bastard Boys* (Greg Combet – AFI Nomination Best Actor), *Ghost Rider* (Sony Pictures) and *True Love* and *Chaos*.

Paul David-Goddard has a BA in Theatre from Curtin University. Paul works regularly as a voiceover artist for TV, film and radio with recent credits including the English dubs of *Let the Bullets Fly* and the Oscar-nominated feature drama *Mongol* as well as several characters for the computer game *Heroes Over Europe*. He played the lead role in the soon-to-be-released feature film *The Sculptor's Ritual*, and has featured in *Mr & Mrs Murder*, *Winners and Losers*, *Australia on Trial*, *Blue Heelers*, and the feature *John Doe*. He has also performed in return seasons of *Hidden Dragons* for Barking Gecko Theatre Company at the Vancouver International Children's Festival, the Melbourne Arts Centre and the Opera House, and in the critically acclaimed *An Air Balloon Across Antarctica* at the Edinburgh and Adelaide Fringe Festivals which had sell-out seasons and received a Fringe First Award Nomination.

SIMON MAIDEN
PERFORMER

Simon Maiden has built an enviable list of credits across film, television and the stage. A graduate of WAAPA he has featured in films such as *Romulus, My Father* directed by Richard Roxburgh, the Miramax World War II drama *The Great Raid* and the Jason Statham thriller *The Killer Elite*. On television he has been seen in the Network 10 telemovie's *Hawke* portraying Sen. Graham Richardson and *Underground: The Julian Assange Story*, the critically acclaimed Showcase series *Tangle* as well as appearing in a variety of guises in *Bed of Roses*, *Dirt Game*, *Satisfaction*, *Rush* and *City Homicide*. Theatre credits include *Love* by Patricia Cornelius and *Criminology* by Laly Katz and Tom Wright, both for Malthouse Theatre.

NATASHA JACOBS
PERFORMER

Natasha Jacobs has appeared in numerous independent productions around Melbourne for over ten years. Theatre credits include *Roundabout* (MTC), *Colosseum* (St Martins) and *One Cloud* (Theatreworks). Other notable La Mama credits include *The Woods*, *Six Characters in Search of an Author...*, *You're Not the Boss of Me*, *The Killing Fever* and *Dimboola*. She toured for Complete Works Theatre Company in *Cosi* and *The Crucible*, for Lovely Night Productions in *Mr Bleak and the Etryop* and for Regional Arts Victoria with *The Ballad of Cauldron Bay*.

STANDING OVATION FOR
AUSTRALIA'S HOME OF INDEPENDENT THEATRE

In 2013, La Mama will celebrate 46 years of nurturing new Australian Theatre.

Built in 1883 for Anthony Reuben Ford, a Carlton printer, the building at 205 Faraday Street had been used as a workshop, a boot and shoe factory, an electrical engineering workshop and a silk underwear factory before becoming a theatre in 1967. La Mama was established by Betty Burstall and modelled on experimental theatre activities at La MaMa E.T.C., New York. Jack Hibberd's play *Three Old Friends* was the first play performed in the tiny space.

Since that time the crowded intimacy of La Mama has provided welcome opportunities to a host of playwrights, actors, directors, technicians, film-makers, poets and comedians, such as David Williamson, Barry Dickins, John Romeril, Tes Lyssiotis, Lloyd Jones, Arthur and Corinne Cantrill, Judith Lucy, Richard Frankland, Julia Zemiro, and Cate Blanchett... the list of those who have been nurtured there is long.

Under the capable care of Liz Jones (Artistic Director since 1976), and her La Mama team, more than 50 productions are now produced annually at La Mama, and at our second performance venue, the refurbished La Mama Courthouse, 349 Drummond Street. An ever-increasing audience is drawn not only from the Carlton and Melbourne University environs, but from far and wide across the country.

'I set La Mama up, as a space for writers and directors to perform in but also it was a space where people came, as audience, to participate in the creative experiment.'

—Betty Burstall, 1987, Artistic Director of La Mama 1967-76

'Much will be said of La Mama's role in developing a new generation of Australian writing. However, in considering policies and personalities, one should not forget the nature of the space and its impact in making possible performances that would be lost in a large theatre. It gave performances the intimacy of the cinema close-up with the exciting immediacy of the live theatre and the warmth of the coffee lounge.'

—Daryl Wilkinson, 1986, Director
From *La Mama... The story of a Theatre*

La Mama Theatre—which, on various occasions, has been called headquarters, the source, the shopfront and the birthplace of Australian theatre—was classified by the National Trust in 1999.

'The two story brick building is of State cultural significance because it has been occupied by La Mama Theatre... The building is indelibly associated with the performance arts and is a rare manifestation of an experimental theatre in Australia...'

—National Trust Classification Report

When it comes to grassroots Melbourne theatre, La Mama in Carlton is like the 60GB iPod – small, subtle, but containing a whole lot more than you might expect.

—John Bailey, The *Age*. E.G. 29/06/05

La Mama produces work from two venues: 205 Faraday Street, Carlton (opposite top), and at the La Mama Courthouse, 349 Drummond Street, Carlton.

For current La Mama productions and events, see www.lamama.com.au.